Empty Spaces, Empty Places

Three Lenten Dramas

Constance Sorenson
and
Ron Lavin

CSS Publishing Company, Inc., Lima, Ohio

EMPTY SPACES, EMPTY PLACES

For more information about CSS Publishing Company resources, visit our website at www.csspub.com.

ISBN 0-7880-1788-8   PRINTED IN U.S.A.

To the One who
fills our empty spaces,
Our Lord and Savior,
Jesus Christ

Table Of Contents

Empty Spaces, Empty Places

Characters:
Narrator
Reporter
Innkeeper's Wife
Centurion
Mary Magdalene

Scene I: Bethlehem — Interview with Innkeeper's Wife
Scene II: Calvary — Interview with Centurion
Scene III: The Empty Tomb — Interview with Mary Magdalene

Narrator: Tonight we want you to use your imagination. Imagine that we can go back in time to Bethlehem and Jerusalem in the year 40 A.D. It is a few years after the crucifixion of Jesus Christ. A reporter from the *Orange County Times* [use a newspaper from your area] has been given an assignment to take the time machine back and talk to the people who witnessed the birth, death, and resurrection of Jesus Christ. The first place he will visit is Bethlehem where Jesus was born. The manger has been empty for many years, yet it is a place people still come to visit. Why do we go to an empty place? What draws us to it? Maybe our reporter will be able to shed some light on these questions.

Scene I

Reporter: Wow! (*Looks around*) No matter how many times I do this I am still amazed! Going back in time! It blows my mind. (*Walks around*) Well, better get to work. (*Looks at a note pad*) Let's see, the address I have here is the "inn at the end of the street!"

7

Come on, what is this? How am I going to find the "inn at the end of the street"? Well, here goes. This is the last house on the street. (*Walks down the street to an inn and knocks on the door*)

(*Innkeeper's Wife opens the door*)

Innkeeper's Wife: (*Frightened*) Yes? What is it? Who are you? You are not from here; what do you want?

Reporter: Hold on, lady. Don't get excited. I'm not going to hurt you. (*Mutters to himself*, Boy, I wish they would tell you how to dress when you take these trips.) I'm a reporter and I was wondering if I might ask you a few questions? First of all, let me make sure I have the right place. Is this the "inn at the end of the street"?

Innkeeper's Wife: (*Still skeptical*) Yes, this is the last inn on this street but what is a "reporter"?

Reporter: Well, it's somebody who needs a few questions answered so that he can report it to those who want to know. Okay? Uh, is the man of the house around? (*Peeks around her trying to look inside*)

Innkeeper's Wife: No, no, my husband is no longer living. He passed away over five years ago. What do you want with him? I am now the keeper of the inn. May I help you?

Reporter: Oh, well, uh, I'm sorry to hear about your husband, ma'am, but, yeah, you might be able to help me. Do you have a few minutes?

Innkeeper's Wife: I will do the best I can.

Reporter: Yeah, thanks. You see, I'm on assignment to do this piece for my newspaper on the birth of Jesus Christ. From the info I was given, it says he was born in the stable located behind your inn. Is that correct?

Innkeeper's Wife: I'm sorry. I'm not sure I understand what you are saying. Yes, we do have a stable behind the inn. Who did you say was born there?

Reporter: Jesus Christ. It was quite a while back. Like over thirty years ago. It was a census year and I guess the town was packed with people from all the surrounding villages. Anyway, this couple came by desperately needing a place to spend the night. Seems the wife was quite pregnant (*Shows with his hands her big tummy*) and they couldn't find a place to stay, so I guess your husband told them they could stay in the barn out back. Does that ring a bell?

Innkeeper's Wife: (*Frowns, thinking*) Thirty years, that is a long time ago. Let me think. (*Long pause*) I do remember the time of census taking when all the people came here to Bethlehem. Let me think. (*Smiles and gets excited*) Yes! Yes! I do remember. Oh, my! That was such a night. We had every room filled. It was very busy. Yes, I remember now. I didn't see the man, but my husband had told him that we didn't have any more rooms available. The man begged, "Please, my wife is going to have a baby very soon! We need shelter for the night." So my husband told them they could stay in the stable. He told them our sheep and livestock were bedded down there, but it would be warm and safe. They were so thankful. When my husband told me later what he had done, I asked him if I should check on them and see if there was anything I could get for them. Some food or maybe the woman would need my help if she was ready to give birth. I went out to the stable later that night and (*slowly and dreamily*) it was the strangest thing. (*Looks into space*)

Reporter: (*Excitedly, with interest*) What was strange? What do you mean? What happened?

Innkeeper's Wife: Well, there she was. (*Pause*) Sitting there on the straw with the baby in her arms. (*Still staring into space*)

Reporter: So she had this baby. What's so strange about that?

Innkeeper's Wife: Oh, that is not what was strange. There were people there with them in the stable. Shepherds. Kneeling before her while she sat there holding the child. Her husband was next to her (*pause*) looking at her and the baby with so much love and adoration. I tell you, I have never seen such love. It was overwhelming to be so close to it. You could feel it! (*Pause*) I guess the strangeness was that those shepherds were there. Where had they come from and why were they staring like that at the baby? (*Excitedly*) A short time later some very important men came looking for the child! They were dressed in fine clothes and said they were looking for a special child. They said they had followed a bright star and it had led them here to this very stable. A star! Can you believe it? They spoke of him as a king! A child born in a stable who is a king? How could that be, I wondered? (*Pause*) Now do you see why I said it was strange? Oh, yes, I remember, that night of long ago. But why are you coming here now and asking these questions? The couple left with the child shortly after the birth. In fact, if I remember, they left quickly during the night as if they were afraid of something. (*Pause*)The stable is once again just a place where the animals are kept. Would you like to see it?

Reporter: No, that's okay. I believe you. Hey, well, thanks for all your time. (*Puts hand out and tries to shake her hand*) Uh, (*uncomfortably*) you've been helpful in confirming the information I had. My boss will be happy to hear I found a witness who was on the scene of his birth.

Innkeeper's Wife: You are welcome. I'm glad I could be of help. It was good to remember that special night. I'm sorry if I was rude to you, but you looked strange. What do you call yourself?

Reporter: George. The name's George.

Innkeeper's Wife: Well, George, I hope you find all the answers you are looking for. Isn't it interesting that strange things continue to happen at this "inn at the end of the street"? Even you, George.

Reporter: Yeah, right. Well, thanks again.

Narrator: Our reporter found the empty manger and heard the recollection of that memorable night yet the question remains — why do we return to an empty place? What do we expect to find? The manger which once held the tiny babe is once again an ordinary feeding place for the animals, yet the specialness of that night lingers on. Do we come to see the empty place and hope that somehow we can be a part of that night long ago? Let's follow our star reporter and see if his next stop will help clarify things.

Scene II

Centurion: Halt! Who goes there?

Reporter: Whoa! Don't get excited. You can put away that sword. I just want to ask you a few questions, if that's okay with you. I'm not here to disturb anything.

Centurion: Who are you? What do you want with me? What foreign place do you come from? I have not seen your kind before.

Reporter: Well, it's a long story and I'm not sure you'd believe it even if I told you. So let's just say I'm from a foreign land far, far away. Okay? But I do have a few questions, if you don't mind.

Centurion: What kind of questions? Who sent you? My lord keeps someone posted here to keep people away. I don't know why the people keep coming here. There is nothing here but an empty cross.

Reporter: What are you guarding if there's nothing here but an old, empty, beat-up cross and a pile of rocks? Who'd want to steal any of that?

Centurion: A few years ago something happened on this hill and things have been different ever since.

Reporter: Oh, yeah? What happened?

Centurion: A man was crucified here. That is not really strange, as many have died here, but this man was different.

Reporter: Different? How was he different?

Centurion: He was innocent. He was not guilty of the crime they said he had committed. He was betrayed by one of his own men! His own people brought about his death and he was hung there (*points to the cross*), crucified like a criminal.

Reporter: Wow! That is something. How do you know he was innocent?

Centurion: (*Ignores the question and speaks about the event*) I remember that day. It is burned in my mind. This man who called himself Jesus said he was the Son of God. He said that he was a king but that his kingdom was not of this world. The soldiers that were with me made a crown for him while they laughed at him. They placed a sign above his head that said "King of the Jews." It was a strange crown made of thorns, and when they placed it on his head it pierced his skin and the blood ran down his face (*stares off into space*).

Reporter: Sounds awful ... but you didn't answer my question. How do you know he was innocent?

Centurion: (*Still ignores question and continues the story of that day*) That's not all. Before they hung him on the cross, the soldiers stripped him of his robe and gambled to see who would win this simple piece of clothing.

Reporter: Why would they want his robe?

Centurion: It wasn't that they thought it had any value. It was just another way to humiliate him. Then the man called Jesus spoke.

He said he was thirsty, but what did we give him to drink? Vinegar! Bitter and undrinkable! Even that small request was denied. (*Pause*) Then he spoke again and said, "Father, forgive them for they know not what they do."

Reporter: Who was he talking to? Who was he calling "Father"?

Centurion: He was looking up at the sky. Speaking to no one that I could see. He hung on that cross for six hours. He spoke again, "My God, my God, why hast thou forsaken me?" The anguish in his voice was horrible to hear! (*Pause*) Moments later, he said, "It is finished," and he died. At that moment the sky turned black as night and strange things happened.

Reporter: What do you mean, strange? If you ask me the whole story is strange. How much more strange can it get?

Centurion: The sky turned dark. In the middle of the day it was as if the sun had been plucked out of the sky. The earth began to shake. The mountains trembled and rocks were rolling and crashing about. People were running and screaming. It felt like the end of the world had come. Then, just as quickly, it became very quiet and still. The people began to leave the hill. They were crying because of this man Jesus whom they said had healed the sick, made the blind see, and had raised a man from the dead. They said he fed thousands of people with five loaves of bread and two fish. Now he was dead. We had killed him. This innocent man who claimed to be the Son of God was hanging on a cross ... dead.

Reporter: Wow! That's quite a story. I guess if I'd been there and saw what you saw, I'd find it hard to forget. But why do you still stand guard here? Why would people want to keep coming here? It's just an empty cross with terrible memories to go with it.

Centurion: It is strange to guard an empty cross, yet I saw him and I heard him. I still hear his voice. You see, I believe him. I believe he was who he said he was ... the Son of God. I believe this place is a holy place. Why do people come to an empty place to remember him? I do not know their reasons, I just know my reason. It is to remember who he was and what he did. An innocent man who paid the price of his life.

Scene III

Reporter: (*Enters finding woman sitting in the garden*) Excuse me, miss. Miss?

Mary Magdalene: Yes? (*Jumps up; a bit frightened when she sees how this stranger is dressed*) Who are you, sir? Where did you come from? Why are you dressed like that?

Reporter: Hold on. Don't get excited. I'm not going to hurt you. I'm a reporter from the *Orange County Times* [use a newspaper from your area]. I know that doesn't mean anything to you. About the way I'm dressed, well, it's because I come from a different time, a different place. But I don't want to go into that again, so let's just say I'm different, okay? But I have some questions I would like to ask you. Do you have a few moments? Would you mind helping me out?

Mary Magdalene: (*Still leery*) What kind of questions?

Reporter: I wanted to know about a man, a teacher you used to follow or hang around with. His name was Jesus. Jesus of Nazareth? Do you remember him?

Mary Magdalene: My Lord! Do I remember him? Of course, I do. Oh, how I miss him. I knew him for such a short time yet he was so near and dear to me. To everyone he met. Did you know him?

Reporter: (*Points to his chest*) Did I know him? (*Kind of laughs*) Well, not really. At least not the way you knew him. I mean I know about him — where he was born, where he grew up, and a little about his years of ministry but I guess I couldn't say that I knew him like you did. That's part of the reason I'm here asking questions. I'd like to get to know him personally. You know, like you did.

Mary Magdalene: Do. Like I do. You speak of him as if he lived and died and lives no more, but that is not true. Didn't you hear? He is alive! He has risen from the grave. I saw him with my own eyes! (*Voice full of excitement*) Sit down, let me tell you. It was like this. (*Stares off into the distance as if seeing and reliving the night*) That night, that dreadful night! But wait, I'm getting ahead of myself. Jesus had chosen men to work with him. Some of them were local fishermen. One was a tax collector. Anyway, Jesus called to them as they were working, "Come and follow me," and they dropped what they were doing and followed him. They went from village to village talking to the people they met along the way. (*Smiles as she reminisces*) The children, always the children gathered around him. He would stop and draw them close. He always made sure he spent time with them no matter how much his friends urged him to move on. He stopped to take time for the children. (*Pauses, still thinking of Jesus and the children*) Oh, I'm sorry. Where was I?

Reporter: (*Checks his notes*) You were talking about the men who became his followers. Are you talking about his disciples like Peter, James, and John?

Mary Magdalene: Yes! Yes! You know them?

Reporter: Not really. I've heard about them, but can we get back to Jesus? What can you tell me about him? How did he live? Tell me about how he got along with these guys ... these disciples.

Mary Magdalene: Most of the time they got along fine. But sometimes Simon, who was a zealot, would get into a political discussion with Jesus and the other men. Simon wanted to gather the group together and plan how they could overthrow the Roman authorities. He was tired of being enslaved to Rome. Of course, Jesus didn't help Simon's cause when he would say things like "render to Caesar the things that are Caesar's" or "my kingdom is not of this world." The disciples did not understand him. I can admit it now. (*Hangs head sheepishly*) I didn't understand him then either.

Reporter: But you do understand now?

Mary Magdalene: Oh, yes! We knew he was different and special. Yet we couldn't put our finger on what it was. He was a rabboni, a teacher. Some thought he was a prophet. When he said things like "the kingdom of God is at hand" or "my Father in heaven," we didn't know what to make of it. Some of the Pharisees and leaders of the temple called it blasphemy. But they really didn't know him either. (*Pause*) He was a strong man yet gentle and comforting. He would often go off by himself. When I asked where he was going, he said he needed time to be alone to pray and speak with his Father. His Father! Can you imagine that? Having such a close relationship with the Lord that you can call him Father? I could tell that his time alone was very important for him. Many times I wanted to ask if I could go with him but I sensed his need for some quiet time.

Reporter: Would he be gone long? Did he always go alone?

Mary Magdalene: Sometimes he went alone and would return after a few hours. Only one time did he take anyone with him and that was on that horrible night. (*Remembering*) He had dinner with the disciples and then they went to Gethsemane because he wanted to pray. He asked them to wait near the entrance while he went on deeper into the garden to be alone. When he returned they had fallen asleep. I guess the dinner and the wine had its effect. Suddenly loud voices were heard in the garden. Roman soldiers carrying torches came with Judas, one of his close friends. Judas came out of the crowd of Romans and kissed Jesus. This was a sign to let the soldiers know which one of the disciples Jesus was. (*Cries excitedly*) It was horrible. Peter tried to fight back. In fact, he cut off one of the soldier's ears! Jesus told him not to fight. He had been trying to tell us all along what was going to happen but we didn't listen. (*Begins to weep*)

Reporter: I'm sorry. It must be painful to remember.

Mary Magdalene: Yes. They treated him so unjustly. He had three trials in the middle of the night! How unfair! They beat him! Yet he didn't fight back. His words echo in my ears, "My kingdom is not of this world." Still we did not understand. Then that long walk down the street called Via Dolorosa, the way of suffering, carrying that awful cross of execution. He stumbled and fell. He was bleeding yet no one reached out to help him. No one, not his friends or the disciples. Not even me. We were afraid! Afraid of what the Romans would do to us. Look what they were doing to him and he was innocent! Innocent yet they had asked Pilate to crucify him! We were scared and in shock as our beloved friend and comforter, our teacher and healer, was on his way to die. To die like a criminal. (*Cries*) It was bad, so bad.

Reporter: It sounds awful yet I don't understand why his friends and the many people he had healed and befriended didn't try to interfere and save him. Yeah, you were all afraid but he was on his way to be killed!

Mary Magdalene: I know. As I remember it, I asked myself that same question. Yet he told us he was here to fulfill the prophecy of old. Again, we did not understand him or his mission.

Reporter: Please go on with what you do remember and what you mean about his "mission"?

Mary Magdalene: One of his best friends, his mother, and I went to see him as he hung there on the cross. He was dying yet all we could do was sit at his feet and cry. Were we crying for him and his pain? Or were we crying for our loss? At the time, I was numb and didn't think about why. I just kept sobbing.

Reporter: Why do you come here now? As you said, he is risen, he's alive. All that is left here in the garden is his empty tomb. And what about his mission?

Mary Magdalene: Yes, you are right. *He is risen* and all that is left here is an empty tomb. But this is where I came that early morning after the Sabbath. I came to anoint his body but the stone had been rolled away. Men dressed in white were there telling us not to be afraid but I screamed because I thought the Romans had stolen his body and we would not be able to bury him properly.

Reporter: So, what had happened to his body?

Mary Magdalene: He had risen! The angels had rolled the stone away and he walked out!

Reporter: Wow! That is quite a story! Unbelievable!

Mary Magdalene: As I sat there crying, I heard someone call my name. I thought it was the gardener but when I looked up, there he was, my Lord! Alive! I ran to him and fell at his feel weeping with joy! (*Pause*) He reached down and grabbed my hand and helped me up. Then he told me to go and tell the disciples what I had seen.

Reporter: (*Caught up in the story*) Did you go? Did you leave him and go find his friends?

Mary Magdalene: Yes, I did. And I have been telling everyone ever since that day! He is risen! He is alive! (*Pauses, looks at George*) Now, do you understand why I come back here?

Reporter: Well, yeah. I guess. It's a day worth remembering.

Mary Magdalene: Yes, I like to remember all that he did while he was with us teaching and healing. I also come here to celebrate his resurrection. Because he lives, I live.

Reporter: I'm not sure I follow that part.

Mary Magdalene: He is my Savior. He died for my sins and yours. He overcame death and lives *now*. He promised that we, too, would live again and be with him forever.

Reporter: Hmm. Very interesting. I may need to think about that a while. Thank you for the information. You've been very helpful. Well, I'd better be getting back. Thanks again. You take care now. *(Shakes his head while moving away from Mary)*

Narrator: George did spend some time thinking about all that he had seen and heard. He began to understand why people visit empty places as he recognized the need we all have to fill the empty spaces in our lives. We try to fill them with all sorts of things: work, family, power, success, cars, and material things. These things don't satisfy or fulfill us. Do you have empty spaces in your life? With what do you try to fill them?

Filling In The Empty Spaces:
The Soldier

Character:
The Soldier

"I hope this blasted Jewish thing doesn't last too long. I've got things to do, people to see."

These were my thoughts as I was waiting for the criminals. I am a Roman soldier and part of my job is to help with the crucifixion of criminals. My name is not important, but what happened to me is important, and I'd like to tell you about it.

The Walk

I remember how they walked along the road with the people watching them. Some of the people looked sorry for them. Others enjoyed the cross-carrying ceremony as much as they enjoyed a parade. "What is that thing that the last man has on his head?" I asked. It almost looked like a king's crown, except that it was made out of thorns. All three men looked like they were beaten before they began this long walk of death. They looked very tired, but the first two exchanged jeers with the people in the crowd who threw words and stones at them. The last man was different.

I remember when the last man fell. He didn't look like a weakling. He was thin, but he possessed a wirey strength. The whippings must have been too much for him. Yet, it looked like he was actually reaching for the cross, as if he wanted to carry it and be crucified. His strength had left him. We drafted an onlooker to carry his cross.

"He is more willing to be crucified than any other criminal I've ever seen," said one of my Roman friends. "He looks like a lamb going to the slaughter." We laughed at the idea. "A lamb going to slaughter."

The Skull

Then we reached Calvary. The common people called it "Golgotha." Golgotha means "the place of the skull." The other soldiers stripped the three criminals while I prepared the mallet and the nails. The crosses were laid down on the ground and one by one the criminals were stretched out on them. I drove spikes into their hands and feet. It is my job. It is a dirty job, but someone has to do it, and they deserve it. The first criminal freed himself for an instant and punched me in the head in a desperate struggle for life. I cleared my head and pounded the nails all the harder. I almost enjoyed the pounding after that wallop. The second man also struggled desperately. As I knelt near to his face, he spat at me and then bit my ear. By the time I reached the third man, I was as mad as a bull.

I was ready for anything. We stretched him out on the cross. He was limp. He didn't even struggle to get free. As I raised the mallet to strike the nail, I heard someone behind me talking about this man. "The fool! Look at him there. He could have been a great man, but he was a fanatic who didn't take advantage of his natural control over people. He could have been a king. Look at him there."

As the nail entered his hand, he jumped. It was a physical reaction to pain. But that's all. There was none of the usual screaming and cursing. He almost seemed calm. I couldn't believe what I was seeing. No man had ever received the cross like this man. I began to watch him closer.

As I arrived at the second hand, I heard another man whispering, "Isn't he pitiful? Poor man. He was always so good to everybody. There can't be a God at all if such a good man suffers like this."

As nail met flesh a second time, the same thing happened as before. There was a physical reaction to the pain, but this was followed by calm in the face of terrible suffering. And those eyes! They were like canyons. He looked at me and I had the ridiculous sensation that he felt sorry for me.

I began to wonder about this man. Who was he? What had he done that was so wrong? I began to listen closely to what the people of the crowd were saying about him.

One man wept, saying, "I saw him with the little children." How disgusting: men shouldn't cry! Another said, "I heard rumors about him, but you know how rumors are. They said that he healed the sick and even raised the dead. Just look at him now. If he could do such great things, why doesn't he help himself now?"

I progressed to the feet. As I drove the nails in this time, I heard the voice of the woman. "My son," she cried, "the son I nursed at my breast. How could this happen to you? And what of the promise of the angel that you would be great among men?" As I finished the nasty job, I inadvertently turned toward the woman who had spoken. I expected revilings and hatred to pour forth upon me. Instead, I saw a woman who, though she wept, showed a kind of inner peace in spite of all that was happening. She, too, seemed to forgive me. Why?

As I returned to my work, I caught a glimpse of a woman I recognized. She, too, wept. What was she doing here? How could she show this kind of concern for anyone? I listened intently as she spoke. "I never thought he could look like that," she said. "His eyes were always so bright and cheerful and loving. Now they are so heavy with pain. I knew him to be the Messiah. How could this happen to him?" She was tender and genuine. How could she be so soft and lovely? She was a prostitute. All the soldiers could tell tales about her.

As we lifted the crosses into their holes, I was in a daze. Who or what had changed Mary Magdalene?

The Words

My eyes and ears were open to anything that might give answer to my many questions. "Look! His lips are moving. Now we will hear the cursings of a man in the pains of death. At last he can't stand it. He's not so different after all; it just took him longer than the others. These Galileans are tough and they don't feel things like normal people, but at last it has the better of him. At last he will curse us all and I'll feel better when he does." Those were my thoughts in the split second between when his lips first moved and those unbelievable words were spoken. "Father, forgive them," he said, "for they know not what they do."

A dumb silence fell over the crowd. Everyone had heard those words. No one believed what he heard. If the sun had risen at that moment, it would have made a noise. It was that quiet. It was as if the whole world had stopped breathing. I stopped right along with it. The thief on the right had a strange look in his eye.

A Pharisee standing in the crowd broke the silence by whispering to his companion, "See. He tears down our religion. He prays that those who kill him be forgiven. He seems to put Jews and Romans, the righteous and the unrighteous, in the same class. He always did associate with sinners. Where would a religion like ours be if we followed him? It is a good thing that the Romans are killing him. He would have destroyed our religion."

This worked like a chain reaction on the crowd. The silence was broken. The whispers soon turned to talking, then to loud talking, then to shouting. "Come down from the cross if you can, Miracle Man," someone yelled. "He saved others, but himself he cannot save," someone else chanted. The soldiers and the thief on the left joined them.

The other soldiers were getting into the spirit of things. They divided the clothes of the three criminals, but there was one robe left which belonged to the man who was stirring up all of these comments. As they threw dice for it, the robbers were speaking to one another and to the man in the middle. "If you are the Christ, save yourself and us," said the one on the left. The man on the right was angered at the insulting manner of those words. He replied, "Be still. We are guilty. He is innocent." Turning to the man they had called Christ, he said, "Lord, remember me when you come into your kingdom." The reply which he heard caused him to die of sheer joy. "Verily I say to you, today you shall be with me in Paradise."

24

The long hours of suffering continued. It seemed as though hope itself was dying. The man in the middle was all but dead. Crucifixion is slow suffocation. The criminal in the middle pushed up on his feet because of the pain in his hands, then let down because of the pain in the feet. Slowly he was suffocating.

His cheeks were hollow. His skin was dry. He made convulsive efforts to breathe. The bloody hours of pain passed slowly by. It began to rain.

The one who appeared to be his mother and a young man approached the cross. I didn't quite hear what was said, but it was something about caring for one another. As they departed, it grew very dark, though it was only noon.

Most of the spectators began to leave. Some lingered long enough to hear more from the mouth of this so-called prophet. "Eloi, eloi, Lama sabachthani," he cried with a voice so horrible that it defies description. "He calls Elijah," said one man. But I knew the horrid truth. I knew enough Aramaic to translate his words. He had said, "My God, my God, why hast thou forsaken me?" The words struck terror in my heart because I felt that I was part of the reason for this forsakenness. The words were like the blast of a thunderbolt in a canyon, so loud, yet almost inaudible. Lightning ripped across the sick, angry heavens. The earth shook.

Time passed slowly. It seemed as though I, too, was being crucified. The words he had spoken, the things he had done, the people who were there — these things had somehow stirred something which was more than sympathy in my heart.

I was so deep in thought that I hardly heard him when he said that he was thirsty. One of the other guards offered him vinegar on a sponge.

When he had said, "Father, forgive them, for they know not what they do," he was praying for me. I was locked in thought. "I don't know what I am doing," I thought. "Forgiveness? Why?"

In a soft whisper which nevertheless had great resonance, Jesus spoke his final words. "It is finished. Father, into Thy hands I commit my spirit." It was like a cry of victory, not a cry of defeat, like he had accomplished his purpose. He was a corpse. Lightning ripped across the sky.

Several men from the Sanhedrin stayed around to watch one of the guards pierce his side to assure death. Then they, too, left to report the good news to Caiaphas and Annas.

The young man named John, the one who had gone closer to the cross with Mary, the mother of Jesus, said something. I listened carefully as he repeated it evenly three times.

Surely, he has borne our grief.
Surely, he has borne our grief.
Surely, he has borne our grief.

Something was swelling up inside of me. As I watched this man die, as I heard his words of love and forgiveness as we crucified him, as I watched Mary Magdalene and the man's mother, and as I heard the words of John, "Surely he has borne our grief," something was inside me which seemed too big to come out, but too big to hold down any longer.

The soldier at my side was telling me about the beautiful woman he had been with the previous night. I heard little of what he said. Suddenly my face lit up. He looked startled, then embarrassed, as I spoke those words which would not be contained within me another split second. "Indeed this was the Son of God." My soldier friend politely excused himself and began talking to the other soldiers about me.

"He must be drunk," they said as they watched me kneeling at the foot of the cross.

Were you there when they crucified my Lord?

I was.

I did it.

And so did you.

But with God there is forgiveness, even for this. Forgiveness fills in the empty spaces in our lives.

Filling In The Empty Spaces: Saint Paul

Characters:
Narrator (speaks from pulpit)
Saul/Paul (in the beginning, speaks from lectern)
Timothy (non-speaking)

Props:
Two sets of clothing (Saul/Paul); cloak; walking stick; feathered pen (The cloak of *Stephen* becomes the cloak of *Paul.*)

Scene I: Jerusalem
Scene II: Damascus to Antioch
Scene III: Rome

Introduction

(House lights out, except on the side)

Narrator: The importance of Saint Paul as a Christian witness cannot be overemphasized. As an author of anywhere from ten to fourteen of the 27 books of the New Testament, Paul is by far the most prolific of all biblical writers. But Paul's importance goes beyond being the author of many New Testament books. His importance for the forward movement of Christianity is related to his three missionary journeys in Asia Minor (today's Turkey) and Europe.

Saul (Paul's name before he was converted) was born of well-to-do parents in the city of Tarsus in Asia Minor about five to ten years after Jesus was born in Bethlehem. Saul's father was a Roman citizen which meant that Saul, too, was a Roman citizen. Saul was a tentmaker by trade, a Pharisee by choice.

Saul came from a very strict Jewish family. As a young man he was trained to be a Pharisee. He was a strict follower of the law. He studied in Jerusalem under the most famous Jewish teacher of his day, Gamiliel. This training was in the law of what today we call the Old Testament. While in Jerusalem, Saul may have personally heard Jesus teach. He certainly heard of the teachings of Jesus who was called the Messiah by his followers. Saul did not like what he heard, especially after Jesus, this so-called Messiah, was crucified. "No way would the real Messiah be crucified," Saul thought. Saul's superiors among the Pharisees said, "This man must be an imposter whose movement must be silenced." Saul agreed.

Saul gladly accepted the assignment from his superiors to persecute the followers of Jesus. He thought, "They must be eliminated." One of those followers was Stephen, who was arrested and tried in Jerusalem.

Scene I

Saul: Who is this man Stephen whom you have captured? You say that he is a follower of Jesus? Well then, stone him! Make him pay! Let's see if he will still claim to follow Jesus when we get through with him. Here, give me his cloak. I'll hold it while you do the dirty work.

Narrator: The dirty work of stoning Stephen was a slow, painful way to inflict death. Stephen accused the Jewish leaders of wrongly crucifying Christ, just as their ancestors had rejected and killed the prophets. Before he died, however, Stephen prayed for forgiveness for those who were killing him, just as Jesus had done four years earlier. Saul presided at the martyrdom of Stephen, watching his every move, hearing every word. He wondered about what Stephen said.

28

Scene II

Saul: (*On the road to Damascus in the dark, away from spotlight*): I've got to get to Damascus and find those followers of Jesus who have started a church there. We will do to them what we did to Stephen. Then we'll see if they still say they believe in the imposter! This movement must be stamped out now before it grows!

Jesus could not be the Messiah! When he comes, the Messiah will be a conquering hero, not a weakling who gets himself crucified like a common criminal. The Messiah must be a strong political leader like David. We will gather around him when he comes. The Messiah will be ... (*trails off, murmuring to himself*).

(*Pulpit light out*)

Narrator: (*Loudly and slowly*) Saul, Saul, why are you persecuting me?

Saul: Who said that? Where are you? What do you mean that I am persecuting you? I am only doing my duty, persecuting the followers of Jesus. Who are you?

Narrator: (*Slowly*) I am Jesus whom you are persecuting.

Saul: That cannot be. Jesus is dead and gone forever. (*Pauses*) My eyes. What is happening to my eyes? I cannot see. I am blind.

(*Spotlight fades out. Saul changes into Stephen's cloak. Pulpit light comes back on*)

Narrator: Saul was taken to a home in Damascus where a Christian named Ananias was sent by God to care for him, teach him, and baptize him.

Ananias was quite reluctant at first because of Saul's history of persecuting the Christians, but God was insistent that Saul was his man and Ananias was to help him. Saul was healed and helped by God through Ananias. He was also given a new name, "Paul."

The next chapter in Paul's life was a difficult one. Filled with the Holy Spirit and energy to burn, he was required to wait for a number of years before he would be able to pick up the Christian cause and devote his energies to reaching new people for Christ. For Christians, waiting may be difficult, but it is necessary. While waiting in the desert of Arabia, his home town of Tarsus, and the metropolitan city of Antioch, Paul, who was raring to go, was being prepared to come under the lordship of Jesus. Sometimes waiting is the hardest thing of all, especially for a dynamic leader like Paul. Paul studied and worked at his trade as a tent maker. The time was not right for him to pick up the torch for Christ and promulgate the message everywhere in the Roman Empire, but that time was coming.

Christian leaders were afraid that Paul was still up to no good, and that he was just pretending to be a Christian so that he could trap more Christians. Then, along came Barnabas.

(*Spotlight back on Paul, who is in the center aisle*)

Paul: Barnabas was my best friend. For a long time, he was my only friend. He believed in me when no one else did. He stood up for me and defended me when the Christian leaders in Jerusalem and Antioch wanted to have nothing to do with me. Barnabas was my encourager.

Barnabas knew the apostles Peter, James, and John. He knew the other James, the brother of Jesus, who slowly emerged as the leader of the church in Jerusalem. When I started out as a believer and wanted to serve the Lord, it was Barnabas and Barnabas alone who encouraged me and introduced me to the right people. Barnabas was my encourager.

Barnabas led the team on the first of three missionary journeys. After the council of Jerusalem when he spoke up for our cause of baptizing and not circumcising Gentile converts, we departed for Asia Minor to spread the gospel of salvation through Jesus Christ alone. Barnabas was the leader of this team. I was his assistant.

Barnabas was my teacher and my mentor. He pushed me forward. He urged me to use every gift and every ounce of energy in the

Lord's service. He believed in me and saw in me what others did not see. He took a secondary role as I began to emerge from the shadows. It takes a big man to do that. Barnabas was my encourager.

Barnabas encouraged me to accept his cousin Mark as a part of our missionary team. When Mark got tired of the travels and became homesick for his home in Jerusalem, I called him "a mother's boy." I was bitter about Mark's immaturity. Barnabas was more patient. He was more understanding. I am not proud to tell you about it, but Barnabas, my best friend, and I came into great conflict about Mark. I did not want to accept Mark back on the missionary team. Barnabas insisted that we forgive him and let him rejoin us. We split over this issue. I was a hot-headed fool. I laid down the law. I was wrong! I am sorry!

Barnabas took Mark and went one way. I took Silas, Luke, and later Timothy with me and went the other way. Only later when I was in prison in Rome about to die did I reconcile with Mark and thank God for the wisdom of my best friend Barnabas.

Scene III

(*Pulpit light out*)

Narrator: (*Strong, with feeling*) Paul, Paul!

Paul: (*From the center aisle*) Who is there? Who calls my name?

(*Pulpit light on*)

Narrator: Paul, you have fought the good fight for me. For years you have stood up and defended my gospel, even though it has meant that you were persecuted and put in prison. You are now under house arrest in Rome for preaching the truth. Soon you will die. They will run a sword through you and claim that it is the just thing to do.

Think about the future, Paul. Who will carry on when you are dead and gone? Who will keep the faith alive and keep my work going? Think about it, Paul. Think.

(Paul walks over to the lectern and writes with the pen)

Paul: To Timothy, my true son in the faith. Remember what I have taught you. Remember my example. Timothy, my son Timothy, carry on after I am gone.

I am poured out like a drink offering, and the time has come for my departure. I have fought the good fight, I have finished the race. I have kept the faith. Now there is in store for me the crown of righteousness, which the Lord, the righteous Judge, will award to me on that day — and not only me, but also all who have longed for his appearing.

(The spotlight moves from Paul to Timothy, who is standing beneath the pulpit, head bowed. Then the spotlight falls on the Narrator whose hands are raised in blessing over Timothy. Then the spotlight moves slowly to the head on the Christ statue or to a cross and stays there as Paul concludes from the darkness)

Paul: Remember Jesus Christ, raised from the dead, descended from David. This is my gospel, for which I am suffering even to the point of being chained like a criminal. But God's word is not chained. Remember, we can do all things through Christ who strengthens us. Remember Jesus! He fills in the empty spaces in our lives!

(House lights back on)